73 MILES TO EMPTY

Tina M. France

How Visionary Women Refuel When They're Tired,
Uninspired, and Ready to Quit

Special Dedication

I dedicate this book to my precious grandmother, Rosa M. Lovette. She is now resting in the arms of her Lord. She was my very first introduction to God and she taught me what love for God and family really meant. She never missed an opportunity to share her love for the Father with people. God's radiance was always prominently displayed in her beautiful, dimpled smile. She'd be so proud of the woman I am, and I give glory to God for the profound influence she had and continues to have on my life. This book is for you, Grandma!

Acknowledgements

I want to share a special word of thanks...

To My Lord and Savior, Jesus Christ! What a journey this faith walk has been. Thank you for this extraordinary life and for trusting me with the assignment to use my gifts to improve the lives of others! I am forever grateful for your lifesaving and life-transforming power! I'm ready! Let's do this!

To my amazing husband and forever love, Bruce L. France! I thank you for loving me for who I am, for receiving my love and giving it back in return. When you smile at me, all is right with world. I love you more than words can accurately express and I thank you for travelling alongside me on this journey.

To my fantastic children (Jordan, Cameran and Mason), you make me so proud! I am grateful that God saw fit to bless me to be your mother. I cherish every moment we spend together. I thank you so very much for your encouragement and for telling me, "Mommy, you can do it!"

To my phenomenal mother, Janet West, you are the most powerful woman I know. You exemplify the true meaning of faithfulness, intelligence, and grace. I love you dearly.

To my Boss-Lady Sister, Shelly Savoy. Thank you for pouring into me and always encouraging me to be my best self. I look up to you now even more than I did as a little girl. I love you, sis! You make me better!

To my super special Mother in Love, Vernelle France, thank you for accepting me into your family as if I were your own. It means more to me than you will ever know. You're the best!

To the Vessels: (Karen Morant, Shelley Winters, Natarsha Sanders, Jamonica Holmes, Jessica "JRUSS" Gilliam, Vielka Maria Gabriel, Leslie Pinckney and Leslie Brim), thank you for embracing me in sisterhood, providing accountability "in the lab" and encouraging me to keep moving forward. Your impact on my life and ministry has been life changing.

To all of you who will read this book, thank you for the investment. My prayer is that the words inside this book will impact your life to the glory of our Almighty God!

CONTENTS

Preface

When I was eight years old, I attended a revival at my church in Fayetteville, NC. I remember so clearly the night when a guest preacher prayed over me and told me that I would be a preacher. My response? "Yeah, not happening!" I was incredibly shy, and I just couldn't imagine a world where I'd be speaking in front of crowds of people. My Aunt Margaret (we called her "Aunt Mimi", she was also a preacher) prophesied over me and told me the same thing. "You're going to be a preacher". As those seeds were planted, I began to feel the call of God over my life and I realized that there was something to this- that this was a divine call to something bigger.

I was raised in a Christian home so the foundation for living for God was laid early for me. I was extremely active in my church. I was an usher, youth choir member, Sunday school teacher and member of the Young People's Christian League. As I grew older, those foundations continued to help me grow closer to God. I found a church, and I felt my relationship with God get stronger and stronger. I met my husband, Bruce, and we got married and moved to Cary, NC.

In 2007, we joined a local church and really found a place where we felt at home and where our gifts could be utilized. As a new disciple, we were given a Spiritual Gifts profile. My top three gifts were: Pastor/Teacher, Exhortation and Administration. I honestly never had any idea what my gifts were until that point. I just knew I felt God's presence in my life and that there was something more that God wanted for me.

One night, again at revival, my Pastor prayed over those of us standing at the altar. She prayed for me and afterwards she leaned in close and whispered, "God's got big plans for you!" After that point, my journey into ministry began. I was appointed Director of Children's Church and with the help of some awesome people, created the children's church program and curriculum from scratch. I was invited to speak at the Women's Day celebration that summer and then gave my initial sermon on Sunday, October 28, 2007. I was finally a preacher!

Over the years, I was the Nursery Chair. I served as an Associate Minister. I chaired the Evangelism Team. I was a member of the Church Council. I was chair of the Technology Team. I really took my role in ministry seriously and I was fulfilling my call to serve God and His people.

During that time, I felt a personal call to expand my ministry impact and I started a blog called, "Lessons from The Well". It was a collection of personal stories and observations that were intended to inspire readers to get closer to God. I eventually founded, "From the Well Ministries"- an evangelistic outreach ministry. I held bible studies at local Starbucks locations and hosted "The Sanctuary" - a worship service for young adults at different venues in the Raleigh area. I was at the height of ministry and really enjoying being used by God. I was doing all of this while working a full-time 40… sometimes 60 hour a week job as a project manager for a local pharmaceutical company AND coaching my daughter's recreational and AAU basketball teams.

Then, in 2015, all of that changed! I was blessed to be able to leave my full-time research job to work alongside my husband in our family embroidery and screen-printing business AND we separated from our church of nine years. Both of these events were major transitions in my life (we'll discuss them more in a later chapter). But it was during that time that I uncovered some deep revelations regarding my faith and my desire to move forward in the purpose that God had in mind for me.

One of the most powerful revelations was that I was tired! I realized how much I was doing: coaching basketball, preaching, teaching, leading ministries at church, ministering in the community and managing data for multi-million dollar research studies etc. It was taking a toll on me physically, mentally, and spiritually…and I didn't even realize it. Not to mention, it was affecting my most important assignment to be present and engaged with my family. It's hard to be engaged when you're tired! Sometimes, despite the best intentions, doing too much can cause you to become weary and question why you were doing it or if you were really supposed to do it in the first place.

I had begun the uncomfortable journey of processing all of these new emotions and trying to settle into these changing roles. I questioned my ability to hear from God. I questioned my commitment to my husband and children. I questioned my motives. I knew that I loved God with all my heart and wanted nothing more than to be used by Him, but I was unsure of where to go or what to do next. I was learning to adjust to this new life …it was like I was starting over.

Then, one day I was driving in my car and God began a conversation with me that would eventually answer all the questions that were swirling inside my head and weighing heavy on my heart. True to who God is, He taught me how use the faith I had in Him to refuel me, revive me and recalibrate my internal GPS so that I'd know where I was going and how I was going to get there. What God taught me over the next few weeks, were "lessons" I was able to convert into practical steps to help me navigate my way back to divine purpose.

So, I am writing this book to encourage the women visionaries out there like me who at some point in your journey feels tired, uninspired, and ready to quit. I am writing to women who have been told that your impact both inside your homes and outside in your communities have little value, so you work twice as hard trying to prove them wrong. I am writing to women who know they have something to offer the world, but need help getting clarity on what that looks like. I am writing to women in ministry who have had their ministry calling modulated to fit into someone else's perception of what ministry should be. For those of you who are entrepreneurs, athletes, artists, teachers, public servants in government-anyone with a compelling vision that you want to see manifested; I am writing to let you know that during times of transition, fatigue or uncertainty, God can and will show you how to navigate those transitions and position you to come out on the other side with the tools to be successful. He did it for me and my prayer and confidence are that He will most certainly do the same for you. Let's get started…

Chapter One: First Things First

"For the earth yields crops by itself: first the blade,

then the head, after that the full grain in the head."

Mark 4:28 (NKJV)

SACRED SPACES

Before we begin in detail, I want to take this opportunity to establish some context around why you'll hear me talk about lessons I learned while driving in my car.

Have you ever seen the movie, "WAR ROOM"? It's a movie that speaks to the power of prayer. In the movie, Elizabeth Jordan (Priscilla Shirer) is encouraged to develop a lifestyle of prayer to combat the challenges she faced in her marriage. She did it by creating a prayer closet as a sacred space. A sacred space is a physical place where transparency and authenticity in your relationship with God is encouraged and where you're free to cast all of your cares upon Him in prayer.

Well, my car is one place I consider to be a SACRED SPACE. It's a place where I can worship and pray and be transparent in solitude where it's just God and me. Between errands, grocery shopping and morning or afternoon carpool lines, I spend a great deal of time there.

Since the environment I've created in my car is one that has been cultivated to take on an atmosphere where The Spirit of God can be free to guide (John 16:13), regenerate (John 3:5-8), empower (Luke 4:14) and convict (John 16:8); it was no surprise to me that God would use my car to be the vehicle (I know, I couldn't resist) to teach me how to **refuel** and put me back on the path to where I needed to be.

Over a series of weeks, God began to teach me lessons to help me figure out why I was in the space I was in and how to move through it. I was able to translate those lessons into practical steps for moving forward. The reality is that for you, it may not be moments of revelation in your car. For you it may be in your study, or in your bedroom. Maybe you don't have a sacred space at all in this stage of your journey, but you can feel in your heart that there is something bigger that God is desiring for you. Whatever your situation, I pray that the preceding chapters will help put you on the right path to discovering or **refueling** the plan of God for your life.

A Matter of Belief

Dr. Tony Evans, Pastor of Oak Cliff Bible Fellowship Church in Dallas, told a story of a Navy Captain who was sailing and came upon a big light. He thought it was a ship coming toward him. This captain was the highest-ranking officer in the U.S. Navy at the time. So, he got on his bullhorn and said to the ship behind the light, "Move ten degrees south or we're going to crash!"

It said, "I won't move!" You move ten degrees north, so you don't crash!"

The captain became annoyed and said, "Don't you know who I am? I am a captain in the United States Navy. I say you move ten degrees south, so we do not crash!"

The voice came back, "I will not move!" The captain got back on the speaker and said, "Did you hear me? I am a Captain in the United States Navy?" The voice came back, "Yes, but I am the lighthouse!"

You see, in all our lives there must be a supreme authority. There must be something for which we build our theology about life, death, and everything in between. Our faith, or what we believe, must be based on something certain and solid.

I mention that here before we get too deep into the content because what we believe matters. If we're going to **refuel** our passion, then the fuel we use must be based upon a credible, proven source. I say this because many of us rely on our own intellect or the opinions and resources of other people to get us through life, just like our Navy Captain in the story. Can I tell you that while we may think we have the answers, there's no one person or thing that knows us better than the ONE who created us?

Faith in God IS THAT FUEL that energizes us. It's the FUEL that makes our hearts leap when we think about the vision we have for our lives. For our faith in God to work, it must be based on a truth that is universal, well intentioned, and consistent.

God is Universal: God's love and salvation is not assigned to a certain few but is available to anyone who will receive it.

"For the grace of God has appeared that offers salvation for all people"
(Titus 2:11 NIV)

<u>God is Well-Intentioned:</u> God wants what is best for us.

"For I know the plans I have for you," declares the Lord, "plans to prosper you and not to harm you, plans to give you hope and a future." (Jeremiah 29:11 NIV)

<u>God is Consistent:</u> God will NEVER change. Since God has made us with good in mind, his love towards us will not end.

"Jesus is the same yesterday, today and forever" (Hebrews 13:8 NIV)

Now that we know and understand that God's love is available to all of us and that He will never stop desiring the best for us, we can go forward in those universal truths and trust that what He instructs us to do going forward is for our good.

Chapter Two: 73 Miles to Empty

One of the nice features in my car is the gas gauge. When I fill my car with gas, my dashboard tells me how many miles I can drive before I run out. At its capacity, my car can travel up to 400 miles before I need to fill up again. It comes in pretty handy when I'm running low. It helps me decide if I can make it to where I'm going without stopping or if I need to stop and fill up.

One day I was driving, and I glanced at my gas gauge, and it literally read "73 MILES TO EMPTY". I had seventy-three miles until I'd be out of gas and need to stop to **refuel**. It's not like I hadn't seen it before but for some reason, this time it made me pause. I laughed out loud because I thought to myself, "Wouldn't it be great if we had a "faith gauge" to let us know to refuel when we're running low?"

See, in a lot of ways, that gas gauge was the perfect metaphor for how I was feeling in my life at the time. I mean, I wasn't spiritually empty; I still loved God and wanted God to be glorified in my life. I knew unequivocally that God had plans for me and that I had a destiny. At the same time, I recognized that I was not full either. I was tired physically and spiritually and I was uncertain about what the next stage of my life would look like.

The truth is that we all have moments when we feel weary and want to give up. Moments when all of the early mornings, late nights, endless meetings, grueling practices, nay-sayers, and opinion-givers seem to be too much to bear. But what makes your God-inspired vision such a compelling force is that it won't let you give up. When God places a dream on the inside of you, that passion stays with you during those moments of opposition. For many of us, it's all we think about. So, to give up is not an option.

Just in case you're thinking you're the only one who gets tired and weary, think about this: Jesus did too!

39 Jesus went out as usual to the Mount of Olives, and his disciples followed him. 40 On reaching the place, he said to them, "Pray that you will not fall into temptation." 41 He withdrew about a stone's throw beyond them, knelt down and prayed, 42 "Father, if you are willing, take this cup from me; yet not my will, but yours be done." 43 An angel from heaven appeared to him and strengthened him. 44 And being in anguish, he prayed more earnestly, and his sweat was like drops of blood falling to the ground. (Luke 22:39-44)

On the brink of being released into the most difficult season of His life and ministry, Jesus' prayer was to go around it. He was weary and felt ready to quit. But notice his response, ..." Not my will, but yours be done." When you recognize that what you're passionate about is bigger than just you and that God gave it to you as means to heal, restore, lift up and encourage other people, then that's when you understand that giving up is not an option. To move through the weariness, you have to be willing to accept the challenges that come with it and keep it pushing!

As I was sitting there looking at my gas gauge reading, "73 MILES TO EMPTY" in all caps, I heard God say, "What if you do have a faith gauge? What if I can show you how you can tell when you are running close to empty? What if I can show you what to look for and how to fix it? God was saying to me, "lean in and pay attention".

So, over the next few weeks, God used my time in my car, my sacred space, to **refuel** my passion for life and ministry and set me back on my path to purpose.

Chapter Three: CLICK! CLICK!

It was five o'clock and I stopped at the grocery store because I needed to pick up some ingredients for dinner. It was my last stop on my way home after an early day that began with the busy early morning I-40 commute, sorting through what seemed to be an endless amount of emails and putting out project fires (barely having the time to break for lunch). I finished my workday, got back on the road for the evening I-40 commute. I completed my shopping, loaded the car, placed the key in the ignition and I heard- CLICK, CLICK!

Yes, the CLICK, CLICK sound indicating that my battery was dead and that my car WOULD NOT START! My car lost POWER! You have got to be kidding! After a busy day, the last thing I needed was car trouble! Fortunately, my house wasn't too far from the grocery store, so I called my husband for help. He quickly came and we connected my drained, dead battery to his fully powered battery. My car started right up!

Ladies, you know how we are! We tend to have so many things going on at the same time. We are multi-taskers. Often, those responsibilities also include looking after the needs and well-being of others. That's not a bad thing. In fact, that's how God made us. We were designed to be nurturers, givers, and multipliers. Given all that we do, it's no surprise that we can become so accustomed to "doing" that our fuel supply slowly becomes depleted and we become drained with little power to function the way were designed to function. Leading full, productive lives is not inherently wrong. I know many women who have lots of amazing things happening in their families and their careers and yet they are still inspired to keep moving forward with enthusiasm and productivity. There are for sure instances where our "doing" causes us to burnout because we're "doing" more than what we should (we'll discuss that more later). But I truly believe that what separates those of us who are stuck in "doing" and those of us who "do" with "genuine enthusiasm and productivity" is our ability to stay connected to the vision that God had in mind for us. To stay connected - or for some of us, (re) connect to the vision, we must go back to the Vision-Giver. Our God-inspired vision comes from the mind and heart of God. ***He*** is our power source. Our Heavenly Father is our fully charged battery that we need to get (re) connected to so that He can jumpstart us back to fulfilling our purpose in Him.

This leads us to the first needle on what we will call our **VISIONARY REFUEL GAUGE**: *(Re) Connect to the Vision*

In Habakkuk Chapter 2, the prophet Habakkuk had some real concerns and questions for God regarding the future of the people of Judah- namely how God planned to use the Babylonians to bring judgment on them because of their sin. So much so that he spent much of Chapter 1 asking God essentially, "Where are you?" (Have you ever been there? I sure have!)

He questioned God's decision regarding their future, and he questioned what he perceived as God's silence concerning the violence and social injustice they were experiencing. But even in this discourse, God reveals what I believe is a practical approach for figuring out God's purpose for you in any season of your life. And when you can figure out your purpose (the reason you were created), that discovery is what FUELS your passion (a strong enthusiasm or desire for something) and gives life to your vision. So, let's take a peek at Habakkuk Chapter 2:1-3 to find out how we can (re) connect to our vision.

Position

"I will stand like a guard to watch and place myself at the tower" (Hab 2:1a NCV)

In ancient cultures, they would build large watchtowers in their fortified cities and they had watchmen who would climb them so they could see what was coming.

If danger approached, the watchmen would sound a warning alarm and the town would close the gates of the city and prepare for battle.

Prophets were considered God's watchmen. They had to be vigilant in their assignment to watch over the spiritual needs of the people. So when Habakkuk declared that he'd stand like a guard to watch on the tower, he was essentially asserting that he was putting himself in a position to hear from God regarding what was coming next so that he could prepare the people for what was ahead.

So how do we position ourselves to hear from God? By showing up where God shows up. I can't help but think about a young Samuel in, 1 Samuel Chapter 3, hearing the voice of the Lord for the very first time. One night, Samuel heard a voice calling out his name. He thought it was Eli the priest calling for him, but in fact it was the voice of God calling his name. It says in Chapter 3 that… **Samuel had placed his bed in the tabernacle near the Ark of the Covenant of the Lord** *(the Ark was believed to house the very presence of God)*. Samuel placed himself in a position to hear the voice of God because he showed up where God showed up- in the tabernacle where the presence of God was!

What's so powerful about the love and grace of God is that he gives us so many different ways to find Him and experience Him. A great place to start is by connecting with a solid, bible teaching church. By being in the presence of other believers and hearing messages that are centered on the heart of God, you're placing yourself in position for those messages to begin to take root in your own heart and your life will begin to change as a result.

You can also encounter God through His Word- THE BIBLE. There may be some who have not found a church that you attend regularly or maybe you're just not comfortable attending church just yet (...and my prayer is that you will!). I wholeheartedly believe that God will engage us right where we are! Reading the WORD of God is another great way to position yourself to find God. As a matter of fact, John 1 says, "In the beginning was the WORD and the WORD was with God and the WORD WAS GOD! What better place to find God than by going to the source- HIS WORD.

The last one I'll mention is through prayer. Psalm 145:18 reads; *"The Lord is near to all who call on Him, to all who call on him in truth (NIV)".* Authentic conversation with God- that's all prayer is. It's you speaking to God from the heart and allowing the space in your heart and mind for God to respond. What does God's response look like? Sometimes God responds with a tangible impression on the inside where you know you've been with Him- when something on the inside just feels different. Other times, God responds with the answer through a sermon or scripture that brings clarity. God also speaks through other people, by confirming a decision to either move forward with a plan or not. The thing is, the more you pray, the better you'll become at being able to clearly hear and discern what God is saying.

How will you position yourself to hear from God?

- o I commit to finding a local church and attending services regularly. (Make a list of three churches to visit in your community or online)

  _____
  _____

- o I commit to setting aside at least 20 minutes 1-2 days per week to reading the bible. (List the day (s) below)

  _____
  _____

- o I commit to setting aside 10-15 minutes each day to communicate with God and be open to His response. (Indicate what time of day- morning, afternoon or evening each day.)

_____

_____

So, if you want to (Re) connect to the vision, the first thing you'll want to do is get in position! You'll want to get in position, like a watch- "wo" man on your tower, ready to receive what's in the heart of God for you in this season of your life.

Expect

"... and look out to see what he will say to me" (Habakkuk 2:1b NIV)

In full transparency, I think one of the reasons why we have such difficulty engaging with God is because there's a disconnect between 1) what we can see, touch and hear audibly and 2) what we think we know or believe about who God is. What do I mean? When we make a phone call or send a text message, we have every expectation that the recipient on the other end will answer and respond. But somehow, when God is the One on the other end, there is a degree of uncertainty that exists where we're not sure if God is there and if He is, is He listening and will He answer. Oh sure, we may go through the motions and say, "Dear Lord" … but at the end of the day, do we REALLY believe that GOD hears us AND that He will respond.

If we want to (Re) Connect to the vision God has given us, there MUST BE a level of expectation that is rooted in faith and that grows as we take one step after another- obeying each set of instructions before moving on to the next.

The Power of Expectation

Years ago, I heard a story about a drought. It was in a farming community where it hadn't rained in a long time, and things were getting desperate. The ministers decided they were going to call a prayer meeting. They said, "Look, we want the whole town to come to the prayer meeting and bring their religious symbols." So, the whole town showed up for the prayer meeting and people brought their crosses, they brought their Bibles, they brought their rosaries and they all cried out to God. When they finished the prayer meeting, there was no rain in sight, and they all went home.

The next day though, in the town square where they had the meeting, there was a little boy. He prayed, "Oh God, we need rain. God, show your power, and give us rain." As he was praying, the sky got darker. And he heard rumbling in the sky. Then, the shower hit, and it started to pour down rain.

Now, the little boy said the same things that the preachers and members of the town prayed. But when the young boy came, the clouds got dark, and the sky started to rumble, he lifted up the symbol that he brought: an umbrella. He actually expected it to rain. Come on somebody!!

When you position yourself to hear from God and seek Him earnestly, you EXPECT GOD TO ANSWER! Either we believe that God is God- the ultimate and supreme VISION-GIVER or we don't. There is power in our expectation! *Our expectation puts a demand on the source of the need.* If we believe that God is the source whereby we have everything need, that "...His divine power has given to us all things that pertain to life and godliness..." (2 Peter1:3), and we also believe, that "... my God shall supply all of your need according to His riches in glory by Christ Jesus" (Phil 4:19), then our level of expectation should be such that whatever we ask for in faith, we are CONFIDENT that God will provide!

Document

"...write the vision and make it plain..." (Habakkuk 2:2a NIV)

When we position ourselves to hear from God- our Vision-Giver, we gain the clarity we need to accurately direct our focus and attention on what matters most.

God WANTS to engage with us. Think about it like this…. God created each of us with a purpose in mind. As we go before the Lord, we can get answers to our most pressing questions regarding what *He* wants for us at this stage in our journey.

Questions like…

What are my gifts and talents?
Where are you calling me to serve?
Who are you calling me to serve?
What problem was I created to be the solution to?

I believe all of us should have a vision for our lives. The fact that you've chosen to read this book is a testament to the fact that there is vision in you that you have or had that you are seeking to explore or expand.

A vision is like a roadmap that directs us towards who we want to become, who we want to serve, what success looks like and how we plan to do it.

Let's look at my vision statement…

"My vision is to create binge-worthy content that glorifies God and equips emerging, visionary women to use their gifts to improve the lives of others."

Your vision should be clear and as concise as possible and answer some basic questions.

Who do I want to become? *Binge-worthy content creator*
Who do I want to serve? *Emerging, Visionary Women*
What success looks like? *Lives of others are improved*
How am I going to do it? *Equip to use their gifts*

Your vision should be an aspirational statement. It should reflect your ideal scenario for how you want your business, organization, ministry, or project to exist in the world. It should be written, or documented, so that 1) you are clear on your purpose 2) you can communicate your purpose 3) you can act on your purpose. Be sure to also answer those four questions so that you are clear on what you're doing and who you're serving. Now, with that being said, you don't need to be so rigid to have every single one of these questions answered in your statement (although it's ideal). However, it is recommended as a guide to help you move forward with clarity.

Write your vision statement in the space below.

_____
_____
_____
_____

Action

"...that he may run who reads it..." (Habakkuk 2:2a NIV)

Now that you've documented your vision, it's time to do something with what you have written down. Remember the questions we asked earlier?

What are my gifts and talents?
Where are you calling me to serve?
Who are you calling me to serve?
What problem was I created to be the solution to?

Many of us do not know what we're good at or how to put ourselves in a space to highlight our abilities. So how do we figure out what our gifts and talents are? First, let's discuss the difference between the two.

Gifts: Given by God to every believer to serve their purpose (spiritual gifts). Examples of spiritual gifts include teaching, encouraging and serving. (For more information on spiritual gifts, read Romans 12:6–8; 1 Corinthians 12:4–11; and 1 Corinthians 12:28). Talents: Natural abilities received at birth. Examples of talents include singing, art, or athletics.

You can begin by making a list of the things you're good at. Or, you can list your interests or subjects that excite or intrigue you. You could also do a google search for the "Myers Briggs" Personality Test. This assessment can indicate what your personality type is and potential career paths that closely align with your personality. My Myers Brigg assessment indicated that I am an "INFJ" and it was also no surprise that clergy or church worker is listed as a career match! These are great starting points for assisting you in aligning your gifts and talents from a vocational or service perspective.

If you'd like to discover what your spiritual gifts are, you can do a google search for "Spiritual Gifts Assessment" and you'll be directed to answer a series of questions. Once you tally up your responses, you'll be able to determine your gifts. My top spiritual gifts were Pastor/Teacher, Administration and Edification (encourager). It was pretty spot on!

Here's an example of how your gifts and talents can work together to inform your purpose. I saw a news story about the "Soup Ladies" out of Seattle, Washington. They are on a mission to prepare food for first responders, military etc. Their talent is cooking but their gifts are serving- when the two combine it's a recipe for purpose.

So, using this example and what has been covered so far, let's ask the questions….

What are my gifts and talents? *Serving and Cooking*
Where are you calling me to serve? *Seattle, Washington*
Who are you calling me to serve? *Military and First Responders*
What problem was I created to be the solution to (Why?)
Lack of adequate support and appreciation for the selflessness displayed by our military and first responders.

Once you answer the W's (who, what, where and why), you can now begin to define the how. In our example with the "Soup Ladies", the how was to buy a food truck and take meals to local fire stations and other military and first responder locations.

When you identify your talents and join them with the gift (s) you've been given, you have the foundation needed to begin to define a plan to act toward your vision. We'll work on this in more detail in a later chapter.

Wait
"...for the vision is yet for an appointed time..."
(Habakkuk 2:3a NIV)

"But they that wait upon the Lord shall renew their strength; they shall mount up with wings as eagles; they shall run, and not be weary; and they shall walk, and not faint." Isaiah 40:31 KJV

Isaiah 40:31 is such a great promise from the scriptures, isn't it? It encourages us to hold on in the midst of times of frustration and struggle. Despite the hope of this beautiful promise, let's be honest, WAITING IS HARD!

Waiting is hard because we are waiting for something we really want. We are excited and we are hopeful. And yes, we may experience nervous anticipation, but we are still in a positive space and anxious to see that 'thing' we are waiting for manifest. Since we cannot grab hold of it immediately, it makes waiting incredibly uncomfortable.

Although we may experience this discomfort, perhaps we can think about it from a different perspective. Remember in Chapter 1, we discussed the foundational truths that **1) God is Universal, 2) God is Well-Intentioned and 3) God is Consistent**? Well, if we believe those truths- that God wants what is best for us and that fact does not change regardless of where we are in a given season of life- then we must be resolved to believe that when we are in a period of waiting, it is within God's perfect and well-orchestrated plan.

When we approach our season of 'waiting' from the perspective that this delay is for our good, it should prompt us to consider that there is a purpose. There is a reason why God has not allowed us to take hold of it quite yet. Habakkuk Chapter 2 says, **"...for the vision is yet for an appointed time...",** so that suggests to us that there is something happening behind the scenes that is required for the completion of the process.

Timing is everything

This morning I made breakfast for my family. I pulled out my trusty waffle maker and let it get nice and hot. I mixed my batter and let it sit until the batter got thick. I ladled some batter into the hot waffle maker and closed the cover. Now, because I knew the waffle maker was hot, my initial, knee-jerk reaction was to open the cover after only a few seconds because, let's face it, no one wants to eat a rubbery, hard waffle! But the instruction for making waffles said to lift the cover when the steam goes away or is not as heavy. Had I lifted the cover too quickly, there would have been a soggy, doughy mess. On the other hand, had I lifted the cover too late, my waffles would have been too hard to enjoy.

Just like my waffles (they were delish by the way), timing IS everything. More specifically, God's timing IS everything. Perhaps God is preparing another person's heart to help you with your vision. Or maybe God is preparing your heart or your character so when you do take hold of it, you'll have the honor and integrity necessary to keep it. When we step out ahead of God, we can be just like an undercooked waffle- inconsumable and unable to be used to our fullest potential.

So, what do I do while I wait?

Self-Assess

Have you done everything you were instructed to do (we'll discuss this more in a later chapter)? Sometimes, we jump ahead because we want things to happen NOW, but we haven't even completed the assignment given to us.

Leave nothing undone so that you won't miss an opportunity when it comes along.

Adjust Your Focus

I heard a story once about an office building that was several stories high. The people who worked inside would complain about the long wait times for the elevator service in the building. It had gotten so bad that some of the tenants threatened to break their lease and move out. The management team convened to come up with a solution to the problem. All of the structural suggestions were time-consuming and expensive. One guy suggested that the reason for the complaints was boredom. People were bored standing there while waiting for the elevators and it caused them to be frustrated. In an unorthodox move, he suggested that they place mirrors by every elevator on each floor. It was inexpensive and it worked. Soon, the complaints stopped. People were busy looking at themselves and other people and didn't notice how long it took for the elevators to arrive on their floor.

If you're having trouble waiting, *adjust your focus.* If you've done all you were instructed to do, then fill your time with another activity. Perhaps that activity is a hobby or helping someone else reach their personal goals. The more time you spend focusing on what you don't have or why it's not happening for you right now, the more frustrated you'll become. Adjust your focus while you wait, and you'll be surprised at how much time will pass as a result.

Worship While You Wait

There have been times in my life when I've felt like I was going in slow motion. It seemed everyone and everything around me was flying by and I was moving 2 mph.

After I delivered Mason, my youngest son, in December 2008, I experienced complications. During delivery, I suffered a partial tear in my left knee and dislocated my right hip. In a totally separate issue, I spent the next two weeks in ICU after a blood infection nearly took my life (that's a different book for a different day!). Talk about slow motion. I was 32 years old and left the ICU barely able to walk. While I was so incredibly grateful to be alive, I was a wife and mom of now three little ones, and I couldn't even walk without the assistance of a walker. I felt like I was 132 years old.

It wasn't until later that I realized that the blood infection that I recovered from was a bona fide miracle from God. On paper, I should not have made it. God miraculously healed me. And yet, I was still unable to walk. Why didn't God heal of all me?

What I discovered from that experience was that God's interpretation of time was vastly different from mine. **2 Peter 3:8** says, ***"...with the Lord a day is like a thousand years, and a thousand years like a day".*** So, while *I* believed that full restoration of the function in my legs should have happened quickly, that divine delay worked something greater in my heart and built my faith to a level of trust in God that I had not ever experienced before. It was in that season, that I learned what it really meant to ***worship while I wait.***

To ***worship while you wait*** means that despite the discomfort and distress of your current situation, you are demonstrating your dependence on God by turning your heart's posture toward Him. I love this definition of worship from Merriam-Webster's dictionary- "extravagant respect, adoration or devotion". Extravagant respect for me during that time was spending time studying and then reciting scriptures. While I was feeding the baby, I'd recite the scriptures. While I was rocking him to sleep, I'd recite the scriptures. When I laid awake at night in tears and the pain in my hip seemed too hard to bear, I'd recite the scriptures. That was my way of worshipping while I waited. As I recited the scriptures, those promises from

God began to give me peace. Before I knew it, I began to gain more mobility in my legs. I no longer needed to use the walker. Still, I'd recite the scripture, and then soon I was able to walk faster, without the limp until I was able to gain full use of my legs. When you worship God, and offer Him extravagant respect, adoration and devotion, God will send peace and strength. Remember Isaiah 40:31?

"But they that wait upon the Lord shall renew their strength; they shall mount up with wings as eagles; they shall run, and not be weary; and they shall walk, and not faint."

So, worship while you wait, and God will send the strength you need to keep going until it is time take hold of what you've been waiting for.

Okay, let's recap. We're in position and we expect God to speak to us about what He has placed in our hearts to do. We've written it down and acted. After we've done all we can do, we learned to wait on God for the next step in our journey. The last step in Re (Connect)-ing to our God-given vision.

Trust

**"...But at the end it will speak, and it will not lie...
(Habakkuk 2:3b NIV)**

> "I will trust, in the Lord.
> I will trust, in the Lord.
> I will trust, in the Lord
> Until I die"

I had the pleasure of being raised in the south and attending church services in a Southern Free Will Baptist Church. My precious grandma, Rosa Mae, sang in the Senior Choir. She would lead the choir in the refrain above, "I will trust, in the Lord until I die". There was always something so comforting, so reassuring in hearing those words echoing throughout the building with the saints singing and clapping in agreement. The words to the song would resonate so strongly with us, not just because it sounded good, but because the declaration of trust was so incredibly powerful. It was like when we sang it, we meant it and believed it to our core.

I asked my daughter, Cameran, what it means to trust someone. She thought about it but seemed to have difficulty articulating the answer. So, I asked the question a bit differently. I said, "Cam, do you trust ME?" She said,

"Well yeah", I said, "Why"? She then explained, "Well, because I know you. I know that when I tell you something, it stays with you. I know you have my best interest. Also, you tell me things too and you know it will stay with me." (Big grin from mom!)

Simply stated, to **TRUST is to KNOW**. Trust knows the character and quality of a person or thing based on experience and that experience is what informs the foundation of our trust. If we've had negative experiences that harmed us or left us lacking in some way (emotionally, physically, or financially) our foundation of trust is shaky and unstable. On the other hand, if we have had positive experiences that left us feeling affirmed, supported, redeemed, and loved, our foundation of trust is strong and secure.

Our trust in God is the glue that holds the whole process together. It's because we have confidence in God's character and His desire to do what is best for us, that we can boldly and assuredly trust Him to make the vision 'speak' and 'not lie'.

There's no question that God has always been consistent in His love and care for me over the course of my life. But, can I confess that despite that, there are times when my faith is weak? Times when my trust isn't as strong? I'd love to be able to say that I'm 100% full of faith all the time but that just isn't always the case. To be clear, it's not because God failed, but in my 'humanness' I allow doubt to interfere with what I know in my heart to be true based on experience. Doubt can be unbelievably persuasive. So, when those moments of doubt begin to set in, there are some practical things that I do to build my faith back up again. I like knowing that there is something practical that I can do to help me when I'm feeling stuck.

"But you, dear friends, by building yourselves up in your most holy faith and praying in the Holy Spirit. Jude 1:20 NIV

How do I build myself up? I call it the RMD Method.

Remember. Meditate. Decree.

Remember earlier when I said that to *Trust is to Know* and that trust is built on experience? Well, when I want to build my faith, I always begin by going back to my experience.

I will remember the deeds of the Lord;
yes, I will remember your miracles of long ago.
[12] I will consider all your works
and meditate on all your mighty deeds."

¹³ Your ways, God, are holy.
What god is as great as our God?
¹⁴ You are the God who performs miracles;
you display your power among the peoples.
¹⁵ With your mighty arm you redeemed your people,
the descendants of Jacob and Joseph.
(Psalm 77:11-15)

Remember

I know! I know! This sounds extremely cliché, but God has impacted my life in so many incredible ways that I honestly could speak for hours on His faithfulness. So, for me, remembering what God has done for me over the course of my life isn't hard to do. For the sake of this exercise though, let's begin with a short list.

Think of two times when you experienced a hardship or needed a positive outcome in a situation and God worked it out.

Experience 1: The first one should represent a situation that was time sensitive. (Short Term)

Ex: God provided a financial blessing for me to pay my past due mortgage.

Write your experience in the space below.

_____

_____

_____

_____

_____

_____

Experience 2: The second one should represent a situation that was not time sensitive but was something you needed God to work out on your behalf. (Long Term)

Ex: I prayed for the salvation of my daughter and she gave her life to Christ.

Write your experience in the space below.

_____

_____

_____

_____

_____

_____

In Joshua Chapter 4, after Joshua successfully led the children of Israel across the Jordan River, God told them to place 12 stones on the edge of the Jordan River as a call to remembrance and a sign for the miracle that God orchestrated for them that day. When we are intentional about remembering these experiences, it reminds us that if God did it before, He can certainly do it again. Praise God for that!

Meditate

Then, find scriptures that support or encourage you in that area of need.

Ex: God provided a financial blessing for me to pay my past due mortgage.

¹⁹ And my God will meet all your needs according to the riches of his glory in Christ Jesus. (Philippians 4:19)

Scripture Reference:

Write your scripture in the space below.

_____
_____
_____
_____
_____
_____

Ex: I prayed for the salvation of my daughter and she gave her life to Christ.

So, they said, "Believe on the Lord Jesus Christ, and you will be saved, you and your household." (Acts 16:31)

Scripture Reference:

Write your scripture in the space below.

_____

_____

_____

_____

_____

_____

Gather the scriptures and begin to meditate on them. To meditate on something means to ponder, to utter and to reflect. The bible tells us that God's Word shall not return void but will accomplish what it was sent to do (Isaiah 55:11). So, meditate on (speak on, think on, and reflect on) that specific scripture because doing so activates your faith by giving it an assignment. (We will also talk about this in a bit more detail in a later chapter).

Decree

Finally, use the scriptures you've selected to create decrees that you declare out loud daily (or as needed). What is a decree? Dictionary.com describes a decree as 'a formal or authoritative order'. It is also defined as 'an official order issued by a legal authority'. God has given us authority through his son Jesus Christ whereby we have the power to speak to our situation. Jesus said, *"For I did not speak of my own accord, but the Father who sent me commanded me what to say and how to say it. I know that his command leads to eternal life. So, whatever I say is just what the Father has told me say." John 12: 49-50 NIV.* So, when we speak the Word of God, we are speaking life. It is important to remember that the authority is not ours but that given to us through Christ. So, when we decree a thing, the power is in the Name of Jesus! He is our legal authority. *"Thou shalt also decree a thing, and it shall be established unto thee: and the light shall shine upon thy ways." Job 22:28 KJV*

Ex: God provided a financial blessing for me to pay my past due mortgage.

Ex: *[19] And my God will meet all your needs according to the riches of his glory in Christ Jesus. (Philippians 4:19 NIV)*

Ex: "I decree <u>in the name of Jesus</u> that God is providing a financial blessing for me to pay my past due mortgage according to His riches in glory by Christ Jesus"

Decree:

Write your decree in the space below.

_____

_____

_____

_____

_____

_____

Ex: I prayed for the salvation of my daughter and she gave her life to Christ.

They replied, "Believe on the Lord Jesus, and you will be saved, you and your household." (Acts 16:31 NIV)

"I decree <u>in the name of Jesus</u> that because I believe in the Lord Jesus, my daughter (insert name) is saved."

Decree:

Write your decree in the space below.

_____

_____

_____

_____

_____

_____

When you use the RMD Method (Remember. Meditate. Declare), your faith will begin to increase. You are putting your thoughts and your words in alignment with what God has already said about the matter. How powerful is that! This is what I do! It helps me tremendously to focus on the outcome and not let doubt sabotage my faith. It has worked for me and I know it will work for you, too!

As visionary women, God has given us these amazing ideas and plans that we are either in the early stages of executing or deep inside of it and feeling the pressure of trying to sustain and advance it. It can be a heavy thing to have a dream that you constantly think about and wonder – Am I doing it right? Will it be enough? But just because it *CAN* be a heavy thing, doesn't mean it *HAS* to be. God knows who you are. He knows your skill set. He knows your heart. Can I say that despite any feelings of inadequacy we may have, God has equipped us to do the work. We must allow His 'Super' to connect with our 'Natural' and just dig in and do the work. When we do that, God will show up every time!

Chapter Four: Clean Up the Clutter

We are a basketball family. My husband played in an adult league in our community. Our children play recreational, school and AAU basketball. Both my husband and I coach their recreational and AAU teams so to say that we are a basketball family is an understatement. Many times, I find myself in the role of Uber driver with my car packed to capacity with my children and their teammates traveling to and from game tournaments.

Tournament days are usually long from driving back and forth from gym to gym. It goes from early morning to sometimes late in the evenings. As you can imagine, the next day when I get into my car, I find half-eaten pieces of fruit, empty Gatorade bottles, basketballs, sweaty jerseys and just random "stuff" cluttering my car.

I don't know about you, but I hate clutter. Clutter makes me feel as if I can't function at 100%. Clutter makes me feel anxious. Clutter makes me feel ineffective. Clutter makes me feel confined, like I can't move freely.

After the 2nd tournament of the season, I usually realize that that the reason why I'm so frustrated about the condition of my car is because I have not set the proper boundaries. If I want my car to be clean, I must establish that expectation with my passengers. Not only that, I must put a process in place to make sure that my expectations are met. What do I mean? I had to say, "If you eat in the car, pick up your trash and put it in the trash bag". I also placed trash bags inside the car to ensure that what I wanted to see happen, would happen.

During seasons in my life when I felt the most anxious, the most frustrated and the least productive, was usually because my life had clutter. There was a time when I was working a full-time 40-60 hour week project management job, coaching basketball, leading several ministries in my church, doing ministry in the community- not to mention that I was trying to the best wife and mom I could be. It's not that what I was doing was bad, but I had to finally get honest with myself to drill down to why I was feeling so frustrated. It's because I was tired and strained from all the clutter.

I had to take inventory of my life and set boundaries. I needed to change something.

This brings us to the next needle on our **VISIONARY REFUEL GAUGE: Evaluate Your Commitments**

    I had to do a self-assessment if I was going to "CLEAN UP" the clutter in my life. So, I made a list. I categorized my life into four areas: personal, work, church, and ministry. In each of these four categories, I asked myself the following questions. The answers were eye opening!

Personal	Work	Church	Ministry
• What am I responsible for?	• What am I responsible for?	• What am I responsible for?	• What am I responsible for?
• Am I doing this because I have to or because I want to?	• Am I doing this because I have to or because I want to?	• Am I doing this because I have to or because I want to?	• Am I doing this because I have to or because I want to?
• What are areas of frustration for me?	• What are areas of frustration for me?	• What are areas of frustration for me?	• What are areas of frustration for me?
• What do I spend my time on?	• What do I spend my time on?	• What do I spend my time on?	• What do I spend my time on?
• Is there anything I can delegate?	• Is there anything I can delegate?	• Is there anything I can delegate?	• Is there anything I can delegate?

<u>Personal Life</u>

One of the responses to the question "What are areas of frustration for me?" was this feeling like I didn't have time to get all the things done that I wanted to get done. Yet, when I compared that response to the answers to the question: "What do I spend my time on?" I quickly figured out why I was so frustrated.

Apparently, I didn't realize how much time I spent daily watching television. "Scandal" and "How to Get Away with Murder" were two of my favorites. I also LOVE college basketball so if there was a game on, I was all over it. Then there was social media: Facebook, Pinterest,

Instagram, and Twitter (in that order). You see even though I loved to do those things, I had to realize that spending so much time doing those things diverted time away from doing more important things.

Now, let's be clear. I'm a firm believer that you need some type of activity to help you relax and decompress. It is not God's desire for you to work and work and work with no time for enjoyment.

So, I commend the enjoyment of life, because there is nothing better for a person under the sun than to eat and drink and be glad. Then joy will accompany them in their toil all the days of the life God has given them under the sun. (Ecclesiastes 8:15)

So, I made a choice. For me, I decided to give up the television shows (I kept the basketball games because like I said, I'm about that life!). I also decided to limit my time on social media. I stayed off twitter altogether and limited my use of Instagram to official ministry posts rather than entertainment. Those small changes made such a big difference.

Work

One day, I saw a meme on Facebook. It said, "If you don't build your empire, you'll spend your life helping someone else build theirs". I don't know why that particular meme got under my skin so much. So, when I asked myself the question, "Are you working this job because you want to or because you have to?" my first instinct was to respond with "because I have to." It's my livelihood. But that wasn't true. The truth was that I could work for another company or in a different industry altogether. I chose to work there. For nearly well over a decade, I worked in pharmaceutical research helping new drugs get to market. I felt a great sense of pride seeing commercials for medicines that I worked to bring to patients. There came a time though when I had become overwhelmed by the long work hours and lack of flexibility. So, when I asked myself, if this is something I want to do or have to do, I realized that I have the power to change my own circumstance. If I didn't like these things, I could change it.

My husband was an entrepreneur himself and built his business from scratch (proud wife!). He was able to leave his job as a network engineer and work his business full-time. We often talked about what it would be like for me to join him and be a true family-owned business. Well, after I saw the meme and decided that working my corporate job was not something I had to do, that I could change it, we devised a plan to do just that- to change it!

It wasn't instantaneous. I didn't walk into my boss' office the next day and give my two-week's notice (though I really wanted to). We needed a plan. It took us 10-months. I went to work every day and worked hard on my projects. As a matter of fact, when I did put in my notice, my boss noted how honorable it was for me to stay and see my projects through during some of the toughest, most stressful times. I wanted to quit but I also wanted to operate with integrity and see it through until the end. So, I waited ten months. We put things in order financially. We prepared for it. Finally, I was able to leave my six-figure, corporate job and join my husband in our family business. I can't tell you how liberating it was to be able to work for something that would build our family legacy. I will also say this: entrepreneurship is NOT a higher calling than any other job. For me, there was a season of unrest where I knew that transitioning into entrepreneurship was preparing me for the next season of my life. The season that I am currently in right now. I believe that's why the meme affected me so strongly. We have the grace to earn a living in whatever industry God has called us to- whether that's business ownership, ministry, public service, coaching others or using your gifts and talents to help other businesses walk out their vision.

Church

Nursery Chair, Youth Minister, Evangelism Chair, Technology Chair, Church Council, Associate Minister, Worship Leader, Children's Church Leader, Disciple- all of these were titles I held at some point during my time of service at my church at the time. Often, I held two or three titles at once. Now, I absolutely LOVE church. I LOVE worship! I LOVE serving God. That was evident in my willingness to take on so many roles, often at the same time.

When you mix multiple assignments with responsibilities at home and work, it can become quite overwhelming. So, as I completed my self-assessment and realized all that I was responsible for, I had to ask myself did I really need to have so many leadership roles at church and were there opportunities to delegate. Sometimes in church settings (or any setting for that matter where collective effort is needed) we get caught by the 80/20 rule. It often feels like because there doesn't appear to be anyone available to take on assignments, that you should be the one to fill the gap- particularly if you are invested in the vision. If you're unfamiliar with the 80/20 rule it is the notion 80%

of the work is done by 20% of the people. We don't always have to say YES to *EVERY* opportunity. Maybe if we said NO to some things, other people would be free to take on the role themselves (ouch! watch your toes). For me, I think it was the awkward silence that prompted me to say yes to things. But I've come to embrace them and be okay with 'the silence', especially when the opportunity is not my assignment.

Were there tasks I could delegate? YES. Were there roles I could step down from and let others serve in? Absolutely. So, I did and because I did, I was able to free up some space in my life.

Ministry

I knew that God had called me to preach the Gospel and teach His Word. That being said, I also had to ask myself was the ministry that I was doing outside of church and in the community a good idea or a God idea. See, many times just because it's a good idea, we move forward but it's really not what God has specifically called us to do right now. I had to evaluate my activities and ask, "Am I doing this because "I" want to?" or "Am I doing this because God told me to do it- NOW".

Each week I'd do an inspirational video. I also hosted bible studies each month at the local Starbucks. Ironically, both of these activities were ministries that God called me to, but I let slip because my life was cluttered with other things. Doing a self-assessment helped me to recognize that my "busyness" caused me to neglect what God had indeed assigned for me. (ouch!)

The point is that the self-assessment helped me to locate frustration points for me so that I could make the necessary changes and clean up areas of my life that were cluttered. It helped me to set boundaries. Sometimes when we are running low on "fuel" it's because we are allowing inconsequential activities to use more of our time and energy than it should. I'm not suggesting that it's an easy thing to just give these things up. It can be hard to remove things from your life that you enjoy. Though it's hard to do, it is necessary if you want to see real change take place in your life.

If you are experiencing frustration, or anxiety or a lack of productivity in your life, may I suggest that you do a self-assessment so you too can clean up areas that may be causing clutter? Your categories may be different from mine and that's okay. Just use whatever categories are relevant to you and then ask the questions. If you're going to move forward, you have to begin somewhere. You have to know what your boundaries are and then set expectations. You cannot change what you don't acknowledge. So, ask the hard questions and then do the work to CLEAN UP THE CLUTTER!

Chapter Five: Traffic Stop

One day, I was driving down the street. As I approached the stop sign, I looked quickly and proceeded to turn right. To my surprise, I heard a siren and I looked in the mirror, and yep, you guessed it- I was being pulled over by a police officer. The officer walked up to my car and as I rolled the window down, he said, "Good afternoon, Ma'am, do you know why I pulled you over?" "No sir, I don't." I said. "I came to the stop sign, looked both ways. There were no cars coming either way, so I turned." He said, "Well, Ma'am, when you came to the stop sign, you failed to come to a complete stop. You rolled right through it."

Now, in my head I was thinking, "Are you serious? You're going to give me a ticket for that? There were no cars coming. No one got hurt!". As the officer continued writing out the ticket, he explained that even though no accident occurred this time, I might not get so lucky next time. From that moment until this one, every single time I come to a stop sign, I STOP, take a few seconds to look both ways, and then go! Some months after this happened, we had an ice storm. As I was traveling down my street, another car came to the stop sign but failed to stop. They just rolled right through it and almost hit us. My heart was beating so fast! In that moment, my mind instantly travelled back in time and I remembered what the officer told me.

As much as we hate to admit it, there is immeasurable value in following instructions. It may seem harmless to take short cuts or do things our own way, but it usually proves to work against us at some point in the process. If we are going to get back on the path to purpose, we must do what God tells us to do, when He tells us to do it and how He tells us to do it. That's why we begin this process by determining what God has said to us by **(Re) Connecting to the Vision** in Chapter 3.

This leads us the next needle on our **VISIONARY REFUEL GAUGE: Follow The Instructions**

Why is following instructions so important? Let me tell you about a business owner who followed some specific instructions and it changed His business and life forever. We find his story in Luke Chapter 5:1-11 (NIV).

One day as Jesus was standing by the Lake of Gennesaret, the people were crowding around him and listening to the word of God. [2] He saw at the water's edge two boats, left there by the fishermen, who were washing their nets. [3] He got into one of the boats, the one belonging to Simon, and asked him to put out a little from shore. Then he sat down and taught the people from the boat.

[4] When he had finished speaking, he said to Simon, "Put out into deep water, and let down the nets for a catch."

[5] Simon answered, "Master, we've worked hard all night and haven't caught anything. But because you say so, I will let down the nets."

[6] When they had done so, they caught such a large number of fish that their nets began to break. [7] So they signaled their partners in the other boat to come and help them, and they came and filled both boats so full that they began to sink.

[8] When Simon Peter saw this, he fell at Jesus' knees and said, "Go away from me, Lord; I am a sinful man!" [9] For he and all his companions were astonished at

the catch of fish they had taken, [10] and so were James and John, the sons of Zebedee, Simon's partners.

Then Jesus said to Simon, "Don't be afraid; from now on you will fish for people." [11] So they pulled their boats up on shore, left everything, and followed him.

Peter was a fisherman by trade. He had a partnership with his brother (Andrew) and neighbors (James and John). They had been out all night but hadn't caught any fish. Just to add some context, nighttime fishing was the preferred method of fishing. These guys were not novices. They were experienced fisherman. But, on this night, they went out to fish and had no success.

Jesus tells him to go into the deep water and let down their nets (during the day). When they did what Jesus instructed, they caught so much that the boat began to sink. Their business experienced supernatural growth just like that all because they decided to follow Jesus' specific instructions.

Let me tell you another story about a mom who had a vision for the preservation of her family and the financial stability of her household. We're told about her experience in 2 Kings 4:1-7.

The wife of a man from the company of the prophets cried out to Elisha, "Your servant my husband is dead, and you know that he revered the Lord. But now his creditor is coming to take my two boys as his slaves."
² Elisha replied to her, "How can I help you? Tell me, what do you have in your house?"
"Your servant has nothing there at all," she said, "except a small jar of olive oil."
³ Elisha said, "Go around and ask all your neighbors for empty jars. Don't ask for just a few. ⁴ Then go inside and shut the door behind you and your sons. Pour oil into all the jars, and as each is filled, put it to one side."
⁵ She left him and shut the door behind her and her sons. They brought the jars to her and she kept pouring. ⁶ When all the jars were full, she said to her son, "Bring me another one."
But he replied, "There is not a jar left." Then the oil stopped flowing.
⁷ She went and told the man of God, and he said, "Go, sell the oil and pay your debts. You and your sons can live on what is left."

The widow was in danger of losing her son to pay a financial debt after the death of her husband. The prophet Elisha gave her explicit instructions regarding how to keep her son from being given over to her debtors, paying off the debt, while also having the means to sustain them for the future.

Peter was blessed in his business and the widow was blessed in her household because they both understood the value of following instructions. They had three things in common:

1. **They recognized divine authority.**
2. **They did not deviate from the plan.**
3. **They did not alter the timeline.**

When Jesus instructed Peter to "***Put out into deep water***", Peter said, ***"...Master, we've worked hard all night and haven't caught anything. But because you say so, I will let down the nets." (Luke 5:5)***

Did you catch that? Peter called him **Master.** In the Greek translation of Master in this instance, the word used is *Epistátēs*. It not only means master but also *the one who is fully authorized*. Peter had done it the usual way the night before, but he respected Jesus' authority enough to say, "...**But because you say so, I will let down the nets.**" An important key to unlocking the insight needed to reach any goal in life is to embrace wisdom from someone who has the authority and "street cred" to give it. There are times when God will download His vision in our hearts and give us explicit instructions. There are also times when God places people in our lives to mentor us, coach us and guide us along to help us. We don't know everything. Let me say that again for the people in the back…. WE DO NOT KNOW EVERYTHING! A different perspective can open so many opportunities to grow your business, expand your ministry, connect with your community, or relate to your family. Be willing to hear from God. Be willing to take advice from mentors. Be willing to research alternative methods. Once you get clarity on those instructions, follow them.

They also didn't do something contrary to what they were instructed to do. Peter didn't say, I'll go out again but I'm going to wait until tonight because that's when the fish bite. In the same way, the widow didn't say I don't want to bother my neighbors so I'm just going to use these buckets I have stored away in my pantry. She didn't try to conserve the oil and only put a little in each jar. Nope! They both followed instructions. Neither of them deviated from the plan.

Trust me, I get it! There are times when we are tempted to take short cuts because we are frustrated. There are times when we are plain tired, and we want to give up because it's taking longer than we think it should take. But can I tell you that there's no better place to be than in God's perfect will for your life? God will surely lead you in the direction that you should go. We can't move ahead of Him and we certainly shouldn't be behind Him. But we should be in sync and move with the divine flow that exists smack dab in the middle of His impeccable wisdom.

If we genuinely want to see the blessing of God manifested in our plans, we must let God give us the divine instruction we need to be successful. That instruction could either be directly from the heart of God or indirectly through mentors or coaches. After all, He is our Vision-Giver. He is our Creator, and He knows how to perfectly intermingle our thought-processes, our personalities and our skillsets with what will ultimately be the set of instructions He will lay out for us in order to move forward.

So how do we make sure we are doing what we should be doing as it relates to the vision that God has given to us? Write it down! Make yourself accountable. Remember the 'Document' step in (Re) Connect to The Vision? Let's go back to that and figure out how to take what we know and come up with an action plan for moving forward.

So, in Chapter 3 we began by answering these four questions and clarifying our vision statements.

Who do I want to become?
Who do I want to serve?
What does success look like?
How am I going to do it?

Vision Statement

Write your vision statement below.

_____

_____

_____

_____

Let's take these insights and organize them into actionable steps. Answer the prompts below as this will help formulate a list of steps for moving forward.

Who is my target audience (Who will I serve)?
- (i.e. entrepreneurs)

Where do I find them?
- (i.e. Chamber of commerce)
- (i.e. Facebook Groups)

What problem (s) do they have?
- (i.e. disorganized inventory system)

What solution (s) do I have to solve their problem?

- (i.e., Step by Step instructions for managing inventory)

What specific offering (s) do you have to serve your audience?

- (i.e., Book)
- (i.e., professional organizing service)
- (i.e., Instructional webinar)

For every offering, what are the next five steps you need to take to move forward?

- (i.e., Book)
  1. Decide to self-publish or use professional publishing company
  2. Create outline for content
  3. Compose manuscript
  4. Decide on title of book
  5. Create marketing plan

Now list each offering in order of priority.

- (i.e., #1 Book)
- (i.e., #2 Instructional Webinar)
- (i.e., #3 Professional organizing service)

Here are other questions to consider. What is my timeline for completing each task? How often will I revisit my list of action steps (i.e., weekly, monthly etc.). As you revisit each list, update it accordingly and add new tasks as needed.

Now, you have an action plan that is centered around your vision, serves your target audience, and identifies the steps necessary to serve them.

Chapter Six: Time for an Upgrade

I want to tell you about "Darkness". "Darkness" was my beloved Mercedes C230 (yes, I name my cars). Man, I loved that car! It was this beautiful dark, black beauty. It had a sunroof, heated leather seats, power windows and everything I wanted! "Darkness" was perfect for my four-member family. YOU COULD NOT TELL ME I WAS NOT FLY!

Then something amazing happened in 2008 that changed everything! We were expecting a new member of the family! It was an exciting time for us. We couldn't wait for our precious baby boy, Mason, to arrive. He was due December 5, 2008.

Somewhere around July or August of 2008 though, it suddenly came to me that Mason was not going to fit in my beautiful, black beauty! As much as I hated to think about it, I was going to have to trade in my precious "Darkness" for something that would fit us all. It was time for an upgrade.

There will be times in your life where you will realize that where you are going will require you to do things differently. There will be times when it will just come to you that there are some things that MUST change if you are going to "fit" inside of the God-inspired vision you've been given. I am convinced that any shift in your life must begin with a shift in what you think and what you say.

We've accomplished a lot so far on our journey and we're now ready to move to the next needle on our **VISIONARY REFUEL GAUGE**: **Upgrade Your Thoughts and Speech.**

Proverbs 18:20-21 (NCV) says,

> *"People will be rewarded for what they say,*
> *they will be rewarded by how they speak.*
> *²¹ What you say can mean life or death.*
> *Those who speak with care will be rewarded."*

This is one of my go to scriptures because it makes it clear to me that what I say matters. Sometimes, I stop in mid-sentence to change my language because my words are not speaking life. I'll be honest, to do that takes a lot of self-awareness. We can be so casual with our words and we don't realize that what we're communicating is not lining up with our desire. What do I mean? "I'm never going to be able to lose this weight". "I'm just not smart enough to get this degree." "I'm always broke". Have you ever made any of those statements or statements just like them? Each of them represents challenges that are real but when we speak negative words, we increase the likelihood that what we want to happen will not happen. With that said, we can't change our words if we don't get our thoughts right first. We can literally transform our world when we transform our mind.

"Do not conform to the pattern of this world but be transformed by the renewing of your mind. Then you will be able to test and approve what God's will is—his good, pleasing, and perfect will." (Romans 12:2 NIV)

When we think about our God-inspired vision, we must make a choice to either think success or think failure. It may not come naturally, so it will require some intentionality. We need to decide that whenever a negative thought enters our mind, we're going to immediately and intentionally replace that thought with a positive one. I call this developing a *Purpose Mindset*. A Purpose Mindset is a mental operating system that governs how we organize our thoughts in a way that propels us toward fulfilling our life's work. A *Purpose Mindset* is more than just changing your attitude, too. Without a doubt, having a positive attitude is a pre-requisite to having a Purpose Mindset. However, your attitude can change. Someone may cut in front of you in line at the grocery store or step on your toe, and suddenly your attitude changes. A *Purpose Mindset*, however, is a *system* of thinking that trains your emotions and governs your actions in a positive direction.

Now the question becomes, "How do I develop a *Purpose Mindset*?" First, let's think about how we process information. Information is received or disseminated through our three gates: our ear gate, eye gate and mouth gate. In essence, we either hear it with our ears, see it with our eyes or speak it with our mouths. So, developing our *Purpose Mindset* will require that we do things that grow us in those three areas. Let's look at what the scripture tells us.

> *"My son, pay attention to what I say;*
> *turn your ear to my words.*
> *²¹ Do not let them out of your sight,*
> *keep them within your heart;*

²² for they are life to those who find them
and health to one's whole body.
²³ Above all else, guard your heart,
for everything you do flows from it.
²⁴ Keep your mouth free of perversity;
keep corrupt talk far from your lips. "
(Prov 4:20-24 NIV)

Ear Gate:

"My son, pay attention to what I say; turn your ear to my
words." v.20

If we want to develop a **Purpose Mindset**, we must
manage who and what we're listening to. I call it
Constructive Listening. Constructive Listening is
intentionally listening to instruction, advice, or messages
that encourage, empower, and build up. So, what does that
look like?

- Replay recording of you reciting your expected
  outcome
- Rejecting negative information that does not align
  with what God says
- Listening to podcasts and audio books about the
  subject matter

- Listening to praise and worship music that encourages your spirit

Eye Gate:

"Do not let them out of your sight, keep them within your heart" v.21

We must also make sure that we put before us images that will encourage us because what we see with our eyes also impacts our mindset. Creating vision boards or watch YouTube videos that encourage us in a particular area are two great ways to help us with our *Purpose Mindset*. One other powerful exercise is creating a mental picture of the outcome you want to see happen. Take a few moments, close your eyes, and visualize yourself doing what you hope to see happen in your future. God promised Abraham that he would be the father of many nations. God told him in Genesis 13, to look to the north, south, east, and west because all the land he saw, he would be given as an inheritance. Abraham looked out and created a mental picture. I believe Abraham visualized the outcome God was sharing with him. When we do the same, we build up our *Purpose Mindset* muscles!

Mouth Gate:

"Keep your mouth free of perversity; keep corrupt talk far from your lips." v.24

Did you know that your words can impact your future? What we say matters. Proverbs 18:21 tells us that "Death and Life are in the power of the tongue". We have the ability to either speak life or speak death with our words. Knowing this, we have a responsibility to guard what comes out of our mouths. In particular, we have even more of a responsibility to speak life-affirming words concerning the vision God placed on the inside of our hearts and minds.

Knowing this, I put into practice a process much like the RMD Method we discussed in the last chapter. It's a set of affirmations that help me transform my thoughts and direct my words.

Affirmations are positive, personal statements that support and encourage you in a specific area. Affirmations are powerful because they help us to look at ourselves through the lens of God's heart. I believe that our affirmations, just like our decrees in chapter five, should have a foundation from the truths found in scripture.

I've listed below some examples of affirmations that I use to help me manage my thoughts, guide my words and develop a Purpose Mindset.

<u>Daily Affirmations</u>

- I am disciplined and exercise self-control in every area of my life.
- I do not let fear sideline me from what God wants me to do.
- I am blessed with extraordinary opportunities.
- My gifts make room for me and sets me before great men and women.
- Peace reigns in my home and business.
- Everything I set my hands to do prospers and succeeds.
- I seek God first in my decisions and get good results.
- I speak life to people.

Take a few moments to list out some affirmations that you may find useful when trying to get your thoughts and words to speak life.

_____

_____

_____

_____

_____

_____

I speak affirmations over my life so that I can transform my thinking. Anytime a negative thought enters my mind, I immediately replace it with something positive. I encourage you to use them as well because they have been an invaluable tool in helping my faith and getting me closer to my goals.

One of the major lessons I've learned on this journey is that intentionality is key. All the steps I learn. All the advice I gather. All the faith I have is of little value to me if I am not intentional about doing something with them. We must apply the same urgency and deliberate focus to managing our thoughts and words and in turn, developing a *Purpose Mindset*.

Chapter Seven: Plan Don't Panic

Years ago, I was attending bible study at a home in Apex, NC. As I was leaving my home in Cary, I entered their address into the GPS and Siri responded, "navigating to…" and she safely guided me to their location. Now I wholeheartedly believe that God has given all of us gifts and talents to glorify Him and I am no exception. However, on occasion I have been what some would call "navigationally challenged" and I'm still seeking God to release the gift of navigation over my life (lol). Until then, Siri and I have become tight!

When bible study was over, I said my goodbyes and made ready to return home. By this time, it had started to rain. I was halfway down the street out of their neighborhood, and I said, Siri, "Navigate Home"- something I'd done many, many times before.

To my surprise (and panic), Siri was not working. It was now a heavy downpour and again, I said, "NAVIGATE HOME" and nothing. I said it one more time, "Siri, NAVIGATE HOME" and I promise you, without any exaggeration at all, Siri said (in her smug, mechanical voice) "I'm sorry, but I cannot help you right now"- Wait, what? I'm like you really got me out here in the backwoods of Apex and you're not going to help me though? No ma'am!

So, my phone was not helpful, and I had to rely on my already limited ability to find my way home. I'm driving, relying on my vague memory of the turns I made on the way there. I'm driving on secondary roads in Apex where there were especially long stretches of road with little lighting! My panic continues to grow and I'm praying and asking God for help. I finally came to "civilization" with shopping centers and streetlights. I looked to the side and saw a big sign that said, "WELCOME TO FUQUAY-VARINA!" LAWD, HOW DID IT GET TO FUQUAY! THIS IS NOT CARY! I did eventually pull into a shopping center and right there was a one of FUQUAY-VARINA's police officers and he graciously gave me directions to the highway, and I made it home safely.

As I was reliving the events of this experience, I started to think about how unpredictable life can be at times. I mean, one minute, you're doing exactly what you planned to do then suddenly, out of nowhere, the unexpected happens and the direction you thought were headed in, has now dramatically shifted.

No matter how well-laid our plans are, there are times when we come to bumps in the road that we didn't expect. We're now ready to move to the next needle on our **VISIONARY REFUEL GAUGE: Expect Detours**

I mentioned in an earlier chapter, that I was working a 40-60 hour a week project management job. I was a Senior Project Data Manager at a Research Triangle Park Biopharmaceutical Company. I was responsible for leading the Data Management activities for clinical research trials for patients battling autoimmune diseases. I was the recipient of achievement awards for my efforts in leading two separate and complex initiatives within the company. I felt a great deal of pride with the work. There were long hours and many challenges, but it felt worth it to know I was improving the lives of patients. Let's put a pin in this...we'll get back to this shortly...

I also talked about how I had come full circle and began to embrace being in ministry. For years people in my life had encouraged me to follow the call of God on my life. We were on our own in Cary with our families spread between Fayetteville, NC and Winston-Salem, NC. We found a local church where we found a community of people who loved God and loved us like we were family. It was there that I found the courage to accept my call to ministry. It was there that I learned how to create curriculums for youth ministry, organize evangelism events, build technology frameworks for online worship and of course, lead people to Christ!

But my goodness, when 2014-2015 rolled in, I went from living my best life to bawling my eyes out because my life had changed so dramatically. Going to work every day became a huge struggle.

The challenges that existed before became full-on battles. I would wake early before my alarm sounded each morning with the dread of what the day would be like for me. I'd stand in the shower and cry real tears because I just wasn't in the mood to fight those battles another day. Can any of you relate? I knew something had to change.

Then, to make matters worse, we parted ways with our church. It was clear to us that our time there was over. I didn't understand it. I didn't see it coming. I prayed and asked God for answers. I didn't like it. I didn't want to do it. But I knew in my heart that we had to move on. I was heartbroken!

Regardless of where we believe we're headed, sometimes we may encounter roadblocks that force us to take detours. I learned two especially important lessons during this difficult season in my life. First, I discovered that the unexpected didn't have to ruin my life unless I allowed it. Second, I understood that if God permitted it, there must be a reason for it.

Remember in Chapter Three, when I told you about the self-examining questions that I asked myself so I could declutter my life? I determined that my job was something I wanted to do, not something that I had to do. I had a choice to either stay or go. What was critical for me during this time was to 1) recognize the friction point 2) decide what I wanted to do next 3) plan my next move. You see we don't always have control over what happens to us, but we can control how we respond. So, I started to operate with this mantra in mind, "Plan Don't Panic". I refused to feel hopeless like I couldn't get where I wanted to go. It's so vitally important to hold onto hope when we feel like there isn't any and begin to plan the change we want to see.

So, if you're feeling hopeless right now. Let me stop and take a moment to encourage you. I know how it feels to think you're stuck. I know how it feels to be devastated at something that you didn't see coming. What I know for sure is what my sweet Grandma Rosa Mae would always tell me, "Trouble don't last always". It doesn't. It may seem like it, but it doesn't last always. Faith in God and your ability to plan your next move is critical to helping you move from a place of hopelessness to a place of victory.

So, let's create a starting point for how to plan your way out of difficult seasons of transition. We'll use my experience at my job and the process I used as our example. It should go without saying but for the sake of clarity, you should always begin any life planning with prayer and seeking God for insight. Here we go…

1 Recognize the Friction Point
- Challenging work environment and job stress

#2 Decide what you want to do next
- I wanted to work alongside my husband in the family business

#3 Plan the change I want to see
- We moved the business from a storefront to our garage to save money until after the transition was complete and sustainable. (we were able to find a new business location within 2 months after the transition that worked well and allowed us to continue to grow)
- I continued to work until my current project was over so that I could maintain work integrity and not burn any bridges.

If you're in a season of transition, take a few minutes and jot down your thoughts on these three things.

1 What is my friction point?

_____

_____

#2 What do I want to do next?

_____

_____

#3 What do I need to do to get to my next?

_____

_____

The other thing to remember in seasons of transition is that if God allowed it, there is surely a reason for it. When we left our church, I had so many questions. One of those questions was, "Why"? I was a faithful member who served. I had friends there who were like family. Why did we have to leave? Why now?

Then, God reminded me of prayers that I prayed and insight He had given me regarding my future. At that time in my life, I shared with God that I wanted to know more about deeper spiritual matters. I wanted to know more about the Spirit realm. I yearned for more in-depth knowledge about the prophetic because I believed that seed had been planted in me when I was a young girl. Likewise, in our quiet times together, God would show me visions of me on stages speaking to crowds and ministering to people. Admittedly, when God would show me these things, my first thought was, "but what about my church?" "What about my roles as "X" at the church?" "Will they think I'm being disloyal if I pursue the things that you're showing me?"

What I now understand is that my attachment to my church, my service there, ministry assignments there, and family away from home there was causing me to neglect the full call of God on my life. I realized that separating from my church was God intervening on my behalf because

I was too attached, and I would not have pursued what was next for me. I was being disobedient.

That said, I so appreciate the character of God in that His grace is always sufficient. When we're disobedient and stray away from His plan, He makes it possible for us to find our way back. Since then, we connected with a church that has been the biggest blessing to us. We are beginning to build relationships and serve again. You know what else? Our Pastor has the gift of the prophetic and teaches about the very spiritual things that I told God I wanted to learn more about. How awesome is that? I also am still blessed to be in relationship with so many of the family away from family we had at our previous church.

The bottom line is that we may encounter detours. We must plan our way through them rather than panic and remain stuck. We should also recognize that there is a bigger plan at work in our lives and that God always has a reason for the detour. When we shift and allow God to direct us, the blessing that awaits on the other side will be more than our hearts and minds can comprehend. It may not always be the easiest transition, but we can be assured that it is working for our good!

Chapter Eight: Do the Right Thing

Picture this. You are driving down the road and come to a stop light. Then you casually look into your rear-view mirror and discover that a police car has pulled up right behind you. Your heart immediately starts racing and you check to make sure you and your passengers are wearing your seat belts. You think to yourself, "are my tags up to date?" "Are my brake lights functioning?" Then the light turns green and you do a slow start and begin driving right at the speed limit until the police car turns off onto another street or goes around you. Don't act like it is just me!

Come on, be honest! Y'all do the same thing! I found myself doing this a lot. I remember thinking to myself one day," Why do I do this?" "Why am I so concerned? You know that all of these things were taken care of already."

Asking these questions led me to this key observation that brings us to the next needle on our **VISIONARY REFUEL GAUGE: Live with Integrity**.

This experience made me realize that how we live and operate in the world requires purposeful attention. You see, whenever I get into my car, I should always be sure that our seat belts are buckled and that my tags are up to date. I should always have safety in mind whenever I get behind the wheel and I should also pay attention to traffic laws. I should have no fear or anxiety about being pulled over and getting a ticket because I've already done what was necessary to prevent it.

I said all of that to say that living with integrity requires this same attention particularly when we are endeavoring to do something that requires God's blessing and favor. In essence, we ought to live each day conducting ourselves with honesty and holding ourselves to good moral principles that please God and build up His people.

Operating in integrity means that there is a consistent
practice of truthfulness with strong ethical values.

There can certainly be times where honesty is required
for specific situations and we rise to the occasion and stand
in truth in those moments. What I am asking us to embrace
here is a lifestyle of integrity that follows us everywhere we
go. No matter the situation. We stand in honor and truth
whether it's easy or hard. We do the right thing because it's
right and pleasing in the eyes of our Creator.

Why is this important for a visionary leader, particularly
one completing a God-inspired assignment? I believe there
are two primary reasons.

#1 We reflect our Creator.

**"So, God created man in his own image, in the image of
God he created him; male and female he created them"
Genesis 1:27 (NKJV)**

We were created in the very image of God, our Creator.
God is faithful, loving, just, merciful, patient, wise and holy
(just to name a few). We are considerably inadequate in
comparison to God's sheer goodness; however, our desire
and motivation should be to become as much like Him as

possible. What a compliment it is to God when we reflect who He is in our daily lives.

Since we were created in the image of God, then our lifestyles should align with that truth. We cannot sincerely say that we are living with integrity if our actions do not reveal that same truth. How can we say that we are operating with honesty and morality if our interactions with other people are less than honest or immoral? How can we say that we are living with integrity if our business practices are corrupt and do not honor our God-inspired vision or the people we were called to serve?

Let me give you an example of what I mean. There is a business coach and influencer that I follow on social media. I enjoy watching her live videos because they are hilarious, candid and offer business growth content that I find useful to my current business journey. She has thousands of followers and her podcast ranked #1 in her business category. A couple months ago, this business coach sent a note out to her email list (of which I subscribe) and announced on all of her social media platforms that she was hosting a business focused session with Q&A. In her promotion of this Zoom call, she promised that there would be absolutely no selling only focus on the business topic and answering the questions of her audience. I registered for the Zoom. At the beginning during the introduction, she again said "No selling. This is just a conversation". To my surprise, as she gets into her topic, she begins to present "case studies" of clients that completed one of her popular business courses. Now, while she did not say, "Hey, register for this program for $599", her not so subtle inclusion of these "case studies" promoted her course that she had been enthusiastically promoting before this Zoom and enthusiastically promoting after it. She was selling. I'll be honest, it rubbed me the wrong way! It wasn't just me either. Other people on the call had the same observation to which she defended herself by saying that they were "case studies" not sales pitches. To me, that was less than honest. I would have had no concern with the Zoom call that included a sales pitch because she has a course that she needs to promote. I would have registered for the call regardless. The issue here is that she said one thing and did another. Before this happened, I anxiously awaited receiving notifications about upcoming content. After this experience, I admittedly do not tune in is as much. I still think she is super smart! She is knowledgeable about her area of genius, and I still appreciate that about her very much. I do not think she is corrupt or had bad intentions. I said all of this to say that when we are less than honest or when we don't do what we say we are going to do, our credibility could be called into question and our impact and reach affected as a result.

Don't misunderstand, I am not perfect, and neither is she. None of us are perfect. The reality of life though, is that our actions leave impressions that cause people to either connect to or disconnect from our God-inspired vision. My challenge for all of us is to take on the attributes of honor, faithfulness and wisdom as a lifestyle and reflect the character of the one who created us. People are watching and we want to be a good, reputable representative of our Creator.

#2 Extraordinary opportunities come to those who live in integrity

"The Lord dealt with me according to my righteousness; according to the cleanness of my hands he rewarded me." Psalm 18:20

I absolutely believe that God rewards us with opportunities when we are living a lifestyle of integrity. Can I tell you that there is little more frustrating than missing out on an opportunity because we weren't ready for it?

Imagine this. An investor has expressed interest in your business idea, ministry, or project. They have $50,000 ready to sow into your vision. They are ready to sign the contract and begin the collaboration. The last step to securing the deal is for their attorneys and accountants to review your profit and loss statements and other financial information. After reviewing your financials, they discover that you have not been forthcoming about your financial health. So, the deal is aborted.

When integrity is at work in your interactions with people, in your business operations, in your financial matters and every other aspect of your life, you won't need to be concerned that extraordinary opportunities are missed because of a lack of integrity. You won't have to stop and think about the areas of your life that aren't in alignment with the character of God because we are prepared for the blessing that's coming our way. I don't know about you, but I want everything that God promised to me and I refuse to let those opportunities fall by the wayside because of my inability to comport myself with honor and truth.

Let me share a personal story. Our family usually does take-out on Friday nights. I usually order a Cedar-Planked Salmon from a local restaurant and everyone else typically orders Jerk Chicken from a different restaurant. I ordered their food and proceeded to order mine, but they weren't answering the phone. I called several times but no answer. They were open but my assumption was that they were so busy, they were not taking phone orders. I was frustrated and contemplated going and placing the order in person but instead decided to go to another restaurant instead. When I arrived at the second restaurant, they were out of my favorite dish! Really? But, instead of getting frustrated, I was gracious and calmly selected something else. But then, something fortuitous happened! The sweet, little lady behind the counter said, "You know what, hold on, sweetheart, let me go check on something." When she returned, she said, "I thought I'd do one last check and I was able to get you the dish" Listen, I was so grateful! Then, as I was waiting in line to pay for my meal, the owner was directing traffic and I allowed someone to go in front of me. The owner noticed and said to me, "Can I see your ticket?", I said, "Sure". He then folded it up and put it in his pocket, and said, "Enjoy your meal. Have a blessed evening". Huh? I was beyond grateful!!

I'm sharing this story because I really wanted to give in to my frustration. I could have taken it out on other people, but I instead tried to set a good example for my daughter, who was with me, and be honorable in that moment. God honored that decision!! Not only did I get the dish that I wanted, but I was also blessed with a free meal! When we are intentional about getting the integrity piece right, I am convinced that God will reward us with extraordinary opportunities to bless us.

Now, let's pause here and do some self-reflecting. Getting the integrity piece right is an integral part of the whole process. Even if it means asking hard questions and being truthful about the answers, we must get it right if we want the blessing and favor of God to cover our vision.

We are aiming for adopting integrity as a lifestyle. So, let's see where we are on our Integrity Lifestyle Pyramid. Take a moment and see where you fall in one of these three categories.

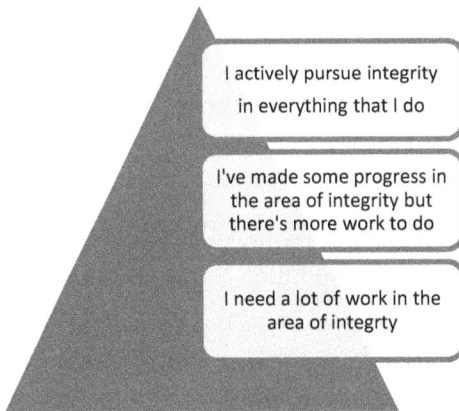

I actively pursue integrity in everything that I do

I've made some progress in the area of integrity but there's more work to do

I need a lot of work in the area of integrty

First, let's isolate some specific touch points that we can identify where we can intentionally improve ourselves in the area of integrity. Are there any aspect(s) of your personal and/or professional life that need improvement in the area of integrity? List them in the most applicable category.

Here's an example.

I need a lot of work in the area of integrity	I've made some progress in the area of integrity but there's more work to do	I actively pursue integrity in everything that I do
• Honesty	• Follow Through	• Fairness

Then, list your touch points related to each category.

I need a lot of work in the area of integrity	I've made some progress in the area of integrity but there's more work to do	I actively pursue integrity in everything that I do
• I use company supplies for my personal use.	• I do not complete work for services I was hired to provide.	• I am intentional about removing bias from my interactions with the people I serve.

List your touch points below.

I need a lot of work in the area of integrity	I've made some progress in the area of integrity but there's more work to do	I actively pursue integrity in everything that I do
• •	• •	• •

With this exercise complete, we've now pinpointed areas that we can work on as it relates to living in integrity. Self-awareness goes a long way in improving the quality of our lives. So, let's take what we've discovered about ourselves and do the work we need to do to make the changes that will make a difference and invite the favor and blessing of God. Let me also say this as we begin to act on these findings. Don't try to do it all at once. We are all human and need to give ourselves time and grace. Select one or two touch points to focus on at a time. I don't want you to become overwhelmed if there are multiple areas that need attention. God will honor your effort and give you the grace you need to keep moving forward. Also, do focus on what you are doing well. It's always a nice motivator to know that we are succeeding in some areas particularly when there are other areas where we may fall just a little short.

In addition to locating ourselves on the Integrity Lifestyle Pyramid, I'd also like us to consider a few more things as it relates to living in integrity.

Identify Your Core Values

Core values are principles that are important to who we are and how we want to be seen in the world. It's like a compass that guide our decisions and our behavior. Take a look below at a list of some examples of core values. This isn't a complete list, but it gives us an idea of what we're looking to define.

Core Values List

Learning	Honesty	Safety	Engagement
Respect	Creativity	Integrity	Diversity
Unity	Fairness	Growth	Excellence
Relationships	Philanthropy	Compassion	Accountability
Service	Loyalty	Leadership	Family
Justice	Courage	Community	Empowerment

Now, select five core values (either from this list or values that are relevant to you) that are important for building a framework for how decisions are made and how behaviors are expressed. My core values, for example, are **Integrity, Making a Difference, Growth, Education, and Inspiration**. Just like our vision statements that we crafted in Chapter Three; these values should inform how we implement and manage decisions going forward.

List them here.

_____

_____

_____

Seek to Serve First

Theodore Roosevelt said, "Nobody cares how much you know, until they know how much you care". A huge part of living in integrity and being successful at what you have been assigned to do in life is learning to build and manage relationships. Remember, God gave us this vision because there are people out there that need what we have to offer. Let me be clear, there is absolutely nothing wrong with success and wanting to be financially prosperous. However, when we prioritize serving over financial gains and notoriety, we win every time.

Do What You Say

Using my earlier example of the "cases studies" vs "sales pitch", it's extremely important to do what we say we'll do. Building credibility with the people we serve is huge. We shouldn't promise more than we can deliver and if we do, then it's okay to communicate and be transparent. We don't have to be perfect, but we can ensure that we do our best to keep our word and build trust.

We must make an intentional effort every day to do better than we did the day before. We should challenge ourselves to treat other people the way we want to be treated. When we do, God will honor our efforts and blessing and favor will follow.

Chapter Nine:
What God Has for Me is for Me

One evening, my husband was driving "Darkness" (my beautiful, black Mercedes C230). He stopped at the convenience store near our house to quickly grab something on the way home. He was alone. He pulled up to the door of the convenience store, hopped out leaving the car running and quickly went inside. Although it had only been a couple of minutes, when he came outside the store, the car was gone. He looked over to the right and discovered that "Darkness" was at a different spot outside the convenience store parking lot with the driver side door wide open and slightly submerged in the bushes.

He was confident that he had closed the door and put the car in park, after all, it was stopped when he got out and went inside. Though he didn't see anyone running from the scene or witness it firsthand, he believes someone saw an opportunity and attempted to steal my precious "Darkness". Who wouldn't want to steal my gorgeous, black beauty?

Why did they change their mind? Why did they exit the car leaving the door wide open behind them leaving the car engine running in the bushes? Could they have had a change of heart?

In the first chapter, we talked about sacred spaces. I shared that my car was a sacred space for me. I had created an atmosphere in that car that was saturated with prayer and worship. I wholeheartedly believe that the "would- be" car thief had no other choice than to cease and desist because the presence of God was so strong inside of that car. God protected what was mine.

I want to take the last moments of our time together to encourage you. God gave you the idea. God gave you the vision. It's yours. It doesn't belong to anyone else but you. Since it's yours, God will make sure that it is safe. Make no mistake, you will have opposition, but despite the opposition, God will cover it with his favor and divine protection.

I've found that there has been one primary threat to what I know is the vision that God gave me to encourage emerging, visionary women to use their gifts to improve the lives others. That threat is INSECURITY. There have been so many times that I've doubted my ability to see this thing through because I doubted the strength of my gifts and talents. To be completely honest, for the longest time, I couldn't really see where I actually had any gifts OR talents. For some of us, it's really easy to see them. For instance, my oldest son, Jordan, is an amazing basketball player. He has the smoothest three-pointer you could imagine. He's a natural shooter! His athletic ability for basketball is evident and unquestionable. My daughter Cameran is a talented artist. She creates beautiful art that I hang on my wall in my office. Mason is academically gifted. I always joke that he'll be the next President one day! My husband Bruce is a creative. He's amazing at creating things. He creates custom apparel as well beautiful, custom furniture. It's obvious. It's tangible. For me, my talents didn't always present themselves so prominently. I am not as creative. I don't build "things". Although I do have a mean jump shot and my lock down defense is top notch (lol), I'm not as athletically gifted. There just never seemed to be anything that I could point to that I could touch, feel, or see that said to me, "Hey Tina, this is your talent".

What God showed me throughout the **Seventy-Three Mile to Empty** journey was that my gift is encouraging people and my talent is teaching. I build up and encourage people through the Word of God. How awesome is that! God uniquely designed me to do just that! Ever since I was little girl, I knew that was my calling. However, I always allowed the enemy to convince me that "these talents don't count". The truth is it does count! They all count! The Bible says,

> "Every good gift and every perfect gift is from above, and comes down from the Father of lights, with whom there is no variation or shadow of turning."
> James 1:17 (NKJV)

They enemy will try to convince you that you are an imposter. He'll try to tell you that you aren't as competent as people perceive. Know this! God has given you everything you need to be successful. If God gave you the vision, He is fully aware of your skillset and your ability to see it through.

I'm going to tell you how God flipped the switch on my thinking on this matter. He took me to Genesis. Take a look with me.

> "Now it came to pass, when men began to multiply on the face of the earth, and daughters were born to them, ²that the sons of God saw the daughters of men, that they *were* beautiful; and they took wives for themselves of all whom they chose.

³ And the LORD said, "My Spirit shall not strive[a] with man forever, for he *is* indeed flesh; yet his days shall be one hundred and twenty years." ⁴ There were [b]giants on the earth in those days, and also afterward, when the sons of God came in to the daughters of men and they bore *children* to them. Those *were* the mighty men who *were* of old, men of renown.

⁵ Then [c]the LORD saw that the wickedness of man *was* great in the earth, and *that* every intent[d] of the thoughts of his heart *was* only evil [e]continually. ⁶ And the LORD was sorry that He had made man on the earth, and He was grieved in His heart. ⁷ So the LORD said, "I will destroy man whom I have created from the face of the earth, both man and beast, creeping thing and birds of the air, for I am sorry that I have made them." ⁸ But Noah found grace in the eyes of the LORD.

⁹ This is the genealogy of Noah. Noah was a just man, [f]perfect in his generations. Noah walked with God. ¹⁰ And Noah begot three sons: Shem, Ham, and Japheth.

¹¹ The earth also was corrupt before God, and the earth was filled with violence. ¹² So God looked upon the earth, and indeed it was corrupt; for all flesh had corrupted their way on the earth.

¹³ And God said to Noah, "The end of all flesh has come before Me, for the earth is filled with violence through them; and behold, I will destroy them with the earth. ¹⁴ Make yourself an ark of gopherwood; make ⁽ᵍ⁾rooms in the ark, and cover it inside and outside with pitch. ¹⁵ And this is how you shall make it: The length of the ark *shall be* three hundred ⁽ʰ⁾cubits, its width fifty cubits, and its height thirty cubits. ¹⁶ You shall make a window for the ark, and you shall finish it to a cubit from above; and set the door of the ark in its side. You shall make it *with* lower, second, and third *decks.* ¹⁷ And behold, I Myself am bringing floodwaters on the earth, to destroy from under heaven all flesh in which *is* the breath of life; everything that *is* on the earth shall die. ¹⁸ But I will establish My covenant with you; and you shall go into the ark— you, your sons, your wife, and your sons' wives with you. ¹⁹ And of every living thing of all flesh you shall bring two of every *sort* into the ark, to keep *them* alive

with you; they shall be male and female. [20] Of the birds after their kind, of animals after their kind, and of every creeping thing of the earth after its kind, two of every *kind* will come to you to keep *them* alive. [21] And you shall take for yourself of all food that is eaten, and you shall gather *it* to yourself; and it shall be food for you and for them."

[22] Thus Noah did; according to all that God commanded him, so he did."

Genesis 6:1-22 (NIV)

Many of us grew up hearing the story of Noah and the great flood. For those of us who haven't, God grew weary of the sin and violence that had overtaken the earth. So, he decided to destroy them and begin again. He told Noah to build an ark.

What I want us to pay special attention to in these verses is the fact that Noah had no idea how to build an ark. He didn't go to college and get his doctorate in Ark Building. All he had was a willing heart and obedience to build the ark according to God's instructions. What was so striking about this passage was the specificity of the details given. God told him exactly what type of wood to use. He told Noah the exact length, width, and height to build it. He instructed him on how many decks to put inside and also how many animals to bring inside of it.

My point to this and the point that God was making to me was that it doesn't matter what idea we have, or project we want to initiate, or ministry we want to begin. As long as we know that God has given it to us, His instructions and guidance are all the affirmation we need to move forward. God knew Noah's skillset. God knew what opposition Noah would face. He gave him the assignment anyway.

God has uniquely and wonderfully made you to do what you do. Doubt and insecurity may come. There may be times when you feel overwhelmed. There may even be times when you will want to give up and quit. Just know that as long as you are connected to Him, He will not allow you to fail. Is it a little scary? Yes, it is. Will you ever wonder if people will get it? Probably. Just keep moving forward. Take one step at a time, getting closer to the goal. You were created on purpose and with purpose. We need what you have for us! Now, go and use your gifts to improve the lives of others! I look forward to hearing your story!

About the Author

Tina M. France is the founder and CEO of Hark the Herald Media, LLC., a personal development company created to equip emerging, visionary women to use their gifts to improve the lives of others. Hark the Herald Media, LLC accomplishes this by creating faith based content that develops leaders in the area of marriage, motherhood, ministry, and the marketplace. She is also a Certified Professional Life Coach who specializes in helping women discover their gifts, get clarity on their purpose, and gain the confidence they need to **Work Their Power!**

Professionally, she worked in the Pharmaceutical/Biotech industry for over 14 years with her last role as a Senior Project Oversight Manager. In this role, she was responsible for overseeing global data teams in Japan, Belgium and Mexico for clinical trial projects that developed new drugs for patients living with Lupus. Tina was honored to be the recipient of three Spot Achievement awards for her work in overseeing the implementation of a strategic partnership

within her department and deploying three key technology
initiatives.

In July 2015, she left the world of pharmaceuticals to use her
administrative gifts in the family business where she serves as Co-
Owner (with her husband, Bruce, who founded the business in
2006) and Business Administrator of France Embroidery &
Printing. France Embroidery & Printing has been a local, family
business for over 14 years and supports established businesses,
churches, schools, sports teams, startup clothing companies and
hobbyists with their company branding and special projects.

In addition to that, Tina answered her call and was licensed into the
gospel ministry on October 28, 2007. She has served in various
ministry roles for 13 years and she has been blessed to speak for
ministries, women's empowerment events and youth conferences.
Tina has hosted bible studies and worship events in her community
as well as ministered words of encouragement through the "Lessons
from The Well Blog" she began in 2009. Tina France has been a
frequent contributor for The Prevailing Woman magazine and has
also been featured in the Faith in Focus section of the News and
Observer newspaper.

She has been married to Bruce France for 19 years and their union
has been blessed with three children: Jordan, Cameran and Mason.

WANT TINA TO SPEAK AT YOUR NEXT EVENT?

Tina M. France has been described as a captivating and engaging communicator who delivers clear, thoughtful, and motivating messages. Tina shares solid, scripture-based teaching with practical, real-world application that leaves her audiences feeling grounded, inspired, and wanting to hear more.

Tina is available for keynotes, workshops, seminars, panels, conferences, and retreats. Her presentations can be tailored to your audience based on their specific needs.

Signature Talks:
Hidden No More: *Find Your Voice and Stop Playing Small*
Work Your Power: *How to Gain the Confidence You Need to Be Authentically You*
It All Counts: *How to Identify Your Gifts When It's Not Easy to Tell*
Plan Don't Panic: *Strategic Planning During Seasons of Transition*
The Purpose Mindset: *How to Think and Talk Like a Visionary*

To book Tina for your event, visit www.harktheheraldmedia.com or email requests to booking@harktheheraldmedia.com.

HARK THE HERALD MEDIA

Coming Soon!

Books
Good Bones: The Seven Leadership Lessons I Learned While Building
My She Shed!

Podcast
The WordGirl Podcast- A podcast for women to connect biblical
principles to success in Marriage, Motherhood, Ministry, and the
Marketplace.

Word Girl University
An online portal with resources to equip and empower women with faith-
based leadership principles to help them in their pursuit and execution of
their purpose.

For more information on upcoming projects by Hark the Herald Media,
LLC, visit www.harktheheraldmedia.com or email
info@harktheheraldmedia.com.

HARK THE HERALD MEDIA

www.ingramcontent.com/pod-product-compliance
Lightning Source LLC
Chambersburg PA
CBHW031043110426
42740CB00048B/1012